Made in the USA
Coppell, TX
12 August 2021

Women Don't Settle! Know Your Worth!

Acknowledgments to my mother, the late *Annie L. Phillips*, and my grandmother, the late *Mattie L. Waters*. To my stepmother, *Patrica A Curll*. To my sisters, the late *Deborah A. White, Shirley D. Edwards, Angelia Burns* and *Karen O'neal*. To my daughters *Tiara M. Parker, Keyiara Gause, Camisha Hollins* and *Crissanna Brooks*, And to my granddaughters *Sydney Britton* and *Mikala Phillips*.

Contents

Introduction

This book is for the Woman who may not have someone that will listen to her talk. It is for the Woman who will not, or cannot, seek therapy. It is for the Woman who feels stuck in a toxic relationship. It is for the Woman who feels emotionally or financially obligated to her Significant Other. It is for the Woman who constantly finds herself in a dead-end, revolving-door relationships, repeating the same vicious cycle over and over and over...

It is for the Woman who lacks the guidance and leadership of a strong Woman of Wisdom.

Woman know your worth! Know what God has for you! Know who you are and Whose you are! We must remember that we are the King's Daughters!

I will praise you; for I am fearfully and wonderfully made:
marvelous are your works; and that my soul knows right well.
Psalm 139:14

Chapter 1

Women, real talk… So many of us today feel like we have to have a man – so much so that we will accept anything, including all of the emotional baggage, disrespect, and drama that he brings into a relationship. But it's clear that this is not describing a real man, and definitely not a King.

Let us talk about some of the concepts of that emotional baggage that he might be carrying. He might have mother issues, meaning she wasn't in his life or she wasn't a good mother. She may have suffered from a drug addiction. She may have emotionally, physically, or mentally abused him.

As a child he may have seen a male figure disrespecting or manipulating his mother. He may have seen his mother accepting this mistreatment. He may think that "if it was good enough for Momma," then all women should probably be treated the same. There are many forms of abuse that can lead to emotional baggage for men, and for women, too. In this book we will examine the baggage the male may carry. These are some examples too look for as red flags in a relationship.

I've heard people say oh you will know how he will treat you by the way he treats his mother. This is not necessarily true. I have seen some instances where the male loved, respected, and adored his mother and still treated his mate like trash; so we can't go by that old wives tale. You

may wonder why I say male and not man? Simply, because a real man wouldn't do the things that are in this book. Therefore, in this book we are referring to a male, not a man, and definitely not a King.

I'm not saying that his behavior could come from his parents alone. It could also stem from a previous bad relationship, friendship, or marriage; but that is still no excuse. He must want to seek help and heal from that pain. Unfortunately, some males just haven't grown up enough to seek that help. If he hasn't then he will continue to inflict pain and misery on someone else.

He may feel so hurt that he will knowingly hurting people just so "someone else will hurt, too." It is very true that 'hurt people, hurt people.' That is still not an excuse! We all can be vulnerable at times and fall prey to the devil. *John 10:10 The thief does not come except to steal, and to kill, and destroy*. In any way possible but the key is to know and understand what is happening and seek help. I'll say it again, this must be HIS desire to do so; not just for the mate, but also for himself. We must remember we cannot change anyone! He must want to change himself. If he does not, that isn't a good relationship and again not worth your time, energy, or space.

Now let's talk about other kinds of drama scenarios. Here are a couple of examples of "Baby Momma Drama." For example Number One let's say he has a baby momma (or mommas). Then every time you turn around she is tripping with issues such as constantly calling, but not talking about the welfare of the child they share. If he is entertaining her and allowing her to disrespect you and your house, this is not a good sign! Yes, they are to co-parent their child, but they are no longer together. There should NOT be any issues regarding

continuous phone calls at all times of the day and night that do not pertain to their child.

Now for example Number Two; the EX-Girlfriend or EX-Wife. Don't get me wrong – they can still be friends. But there is a level of friendship that you can no longer access. Those levels turn into the disrespect of always wanting to see him, or sending very inappropriate text messages, or 'surprise' pop ups at the job.

If he doesn't straighten that out there is obviously a whole other level of disrespect on his and her behalf. I have found out in my years of growing you can't be mad at the other woman. What I mean is that at times she might not even be aware that he is in a new relationship. She could be a pawn in his game as well. But don't get it twisted... She may know exactly what he is doing.

Either way, it is his job to put an end to it. I have adopted a truism which says *if you keep entertaining a clown it will keep performing!* Therefore, Queen, stop going to the Circus to look for your new man! We are too old for that drama and mess! Here's a little hint – some men like it because hurting others strokes their ego or arrogance. This is NOT acceptable! Do a quick self check... Do you feel that is acceptable and allow it?

Chapter 2

When you have a male that runs from woman to woman, never finding his own way in life, who sees everybody else as "ignorant to his situation," that is a red flag! He is probably unhappy with himself. There is probably some emotional baggage hidden within that person. He may have the thought that he is grown, but he is not making mature decisions. This means he wants to "run things" and can't "run" himself. A real King is going to make sure he is straight before he approaches the Queen. A real Brother should at least have a plan or goal he is trying to achieve. Not just for him, but for US as a couple, if he is trying to include you.

Ladies, because we have that nurturing spirit we try to take on that situation thinking we can fix it, tolerate it or even change this behavior. Somehow we imagine we can mold and shape this mole hill into something great all by ourselves. Unfortunately, this can quickly become a mountain of despair and we decide to endure the headache and pain just to say we have a man.

In all actuality we have a child in an adult body and we have become a parent to a supposedly adult. In the relationship the man is supposed to be the head. He is to lead as he is led by God. You cannot teach him to lead. When I was a child , I spoke as a child when I became a man I put away childish things (*1st Corinthians 13:11*). I am reminded of a

song by a group named Switch, titled 'I Call Your Name.' In that song he says, "I'm a man now baby, a grown man!" He goes on to say that he "came a long way" and that "experience taught" him how to hold on to his love. Since that song was released in 1979, I might be telling my age – but, oh well I'm proud of it!

We must understand that this isn't what God wants for us. His word states in *Jeremiah 29:11* "For I know the thoughts I think towards you, says the Lord, thoughts of peace and not of evil, to give you future and a hope." So with that being said, being in a loveless, no foreseeable future, and stressful relationship is not a future of hope nor peace. Remove Yourself!

We do not have the power, time, or energy to change a person but we can change ourselves. We hold on thinking it's going to change and we are deceiving ourselves. I'm going to keep it real with you because I have seen these scenarios. You can't use sex, money, or children to change a person. Sometimes people use those scenarios for personal gain. You might think you are using them or they make think they are using you. In fact, you both are being used and will eventually be used up. So it is a dead end. You should not, cannot not, and would not want to do that. You can't change a grown person. I think I need to say that again, because someone still didn't hear it...

YOU CANNOT CHANGE HIM!

So don't even set yourself up for that heartache, headache, and financial ruin.

Chapter 3

We do have the power to pray, seek guidance, and ask for the spirit of discernment in our relationship. We are seeking to know if it is worth it and if God is even in it. Wisdom is the principal thing; therefore gain wisdom and all thy get understanding.

There are some signs to look for that will let you know if it is not worth it. If the relationship takes away your peace, your time, self-esteem or trust it is not worth it and God is not in it. *2nd Peter 1:5-6* states, "but also for this reason, giving all diligence, add to your faith virtue, to virtue knowledge, to knowledge self-control, to self-control perseverance, to perseverance to Godliness."

Ladies please be knowledgeable about the qualities that a God fearing, good man possesses. We must be very specific in prayer. We need to read the word of God so we know. *Psalm 37:23* states, "The steps of a good man are ordered by the Lord and He delights in his way." If his steps are ordered he will not half step and won't allow you to, either. You both will worship God in spirit and truth and expect the best from God while also giving God your best. If a man is not willing to worship with you in a service, to pray with you, or read the word of God with you, then he isn't the one FOR you.

When selecting a mate please make sure he is a man that can and will pray for you and not prey on you! His word should be his bond. If not, he isn't worth your time or attention. You have to be really strong in your heart and mind watching out for those qualities because God did not make you a play toy. You are fearfully and wonderfully made! He made a good thing when He made you! If you two are not in agreement with that and he feels you aren't worth it, he isn't worthy of you!

Never ever dumb yourself down. What I mean by that is never allow **anyone**, not just a male, to make you think less of yourself and that your opinion and feelings don't count. Do not change what you were doing and do not let him get comfortable with trying to change you to get you to that place. If he is not a man of God he can't lead you because he can't lead himself. He might say with his lips that he has a relationship with God, but the truth of the matter will show in his life his actions.

Trust me when I say that part because I have experienced it. I have had several men that have preyed on me. Read that again. Not *prayed with* me, but *preyed on* me. The main arena used to stalk me was social media. They would get on there, read my profile and some of my posts and the plot begins. Then they jump in my inbox or send me a friend request with, 'oh woman of God you are beautiful and I have been looking for a God fearing woman! I love your post,' and at that time I didn't know any better – just being honest. Ladies, another thing that we really have to do is be honest with ourselves! If not, we end up repeating that same vicious cycle.

Chapter 4

Queens, sometimes we want to look at men with our worldly eyes, and disregard our spiritual discernment. For instance, we meet a good looking guy who seems like he's got it all together. We may allow him into our physical and spiritual space. Then we find he has deceived you with what he thinks you want to hear and see and feel. The right attention at the wrong time in a bored or lonely moment can make you think, 'oh he is the one God has blessed me with...' No ma'am! We get caught up, both physically and emotionally. I'm speaking from experience. Been there, done that, and now writing the book about it!

Some of us women normally operate off of our emotions and some men operate off their ego. That isn't good for either side, male or female. Because when we get tired of waiting on our Boaz we think we have to settle for *PO-az*, or *BROKE-az*, or *RIGHT-NOW-az*. If you find that person makes you more miserable than happy it doesn't matter what you think you are feeling, you must let them go! Desperately clinging to the *FAKE-az* will cause us to miss the real true Boaz that God had been grooming for us. *Isaiah 40:31* "But those who wait on the Lord Shall renew their strength; they shall mount up with wings like eagles, they shall run and not be weary, they shall walk and not faint."

Now let me say just a little more about this. Sometimes we think we have to settle. Sometimes we may think, 'oh he is the one God sent from above.' This is not necessarily true. The devil hears the prayers meant for God and will send you what you asked for dressed as an impostor. Then you get caught up again. I stated that earlier, but I need you to hear me because we will be in that same repeat cycle of hurt and misery.

Therefore we must learn to be patient stay focused, prayed up, and most definitely in the will of God. I won't lie to you, this isn't easy. Don't just accept the first man you encounter because you are tired of waiting on Mr. Right. We think, 'oh it isn't that bad' or 'I can deal with a few bothersome things.' We may even think he will eventually change. Like I said in chapter two, **YOU CANNOT CHANGE HIM!!!** He can and will change his characteristics only if he *wants* to do so. That is why we should know our worth and what we bring to the table. I don't mean only financially, but spiritually, mentally and emotionally.

Ladies treat yourself like a Five-Star, believing that you are the finest piece of work God has created! Please please respect yourself because when you do, that is what you will attract. A real man will always respect you. On the other hand, if you treat yourself like a dumping ground or junk yard then only junk yard dogs will be attracted to you.

Know this you are already complete! You don't need a man to make you complete! When God made you He completed you! Now it is up to you to know, respect, and live like it. I'm probably about to offend someone but I wouldn't be doing God's work if I didn't tell you this. Ladies you do not have to walk around half-naked to get noticed by the right man. If your intention is to just be noticed by any-*thing* that

doesn't value you as a Queen, then that is what you will get when showing all of what God has created to the world.

Let me break that down just little more. Have some self-respect and leave something to the imagination, something for your King to desire. No, I'm not saying you have to wear a dress or skirt to the ground, or a turtle neck covering your face. Your body is a Temple that should be well covered and taken care of with pride. *1 Corinthians 6:19-20* says, "Or do you not know that your body is the temple of the Holy Spirit who is in you, whom you have from God, and you are not your own? For you were bought at a price; therefore glorify God in your body and in your spirit, which are God's."

Now let me also expound on something I said earlier about being spiritually covered. I never thought about this until prayer and speaking with women of God. I was taught about all of the different spirits that you are entangled with when you lie down with a male. You are taking on all kinds of previous spirits and entanglements from previous relationships. And no, everyone is not going to be a virgin. I'm not implying that at all. If so, I would be lying and this is a keep-it-real type of book for my *Sista's*! This is a vice versa situation as well, since we have no clue what type of spirits we are mixing up laying with different people when there is no Godly covenant involved.

Chapter 5

Let me share some of the issues that I had and the devil knew it because he knows our weakness and plays on them viciously. I had a lonely spirit at times and I didn't know that at first. We have to do a self-check AND get in the Word of God AND connect with spiritual people. You have to be careful with that because every spirit isn't a Godly spirit. Therefore the people better be Christ-like people that can help you identify those spirits and take charge over them.

I use to think because a man showed me some attention and told me he loved me he was the one for me. I didn't realize that he knew how to play me. He knew that was what I was looking for; that fairy tale love. We have to be careful because Satan is very crafty! You can find so-called *love* in all of the wrong places. Men can be very manipulating. That is lust, not love. Know the difference! Most of all know your worth! I'm just keeping it real, hoping I can help another sister along the way.

Let's say you meet a man, 6'4", handsome, seductive eyes, and a sexy voice that just makes you melt like ice cream! You think yes-yes-yes! But its a no-no-no! Don't get me wrong, not all 6'4" men are like that. I was taught a lesson by one and that is the example I'm using. Please don't quote me as saying **all** 6'4 men are devils! As a matter of fact, he wasn't a devil. He just wasn't the man God had for me. Before I realized he wasn't I had already started fantasizing about our relationship,

picturing how we would look together. I'm 5'1", and he is 6"4 – I had hit the jackpot! I thought I finally got my Mr. Right.

Well, that went all wrong and I had to realize that looks aren't everything! Trust and believe I have heard women say, "I don't care if he is ugly as long as he treats me right." Ladies are you being truthful with that statement? I'm going to share a couple of my life experiences throughout this book with you. At first I was like 'don't tell these women your business...' Then I realized helping my sisters IS my business, so here we go. I met a guy when I was in my early twenties and he had my nose 'wide open!' That was mister 6'4" from earlier in the book. Honey, if that man told me the sky was purple and the grass was pink I believed him because I was that caught up! That relationship cost me my peace and almost my life because my mind was so caught up with him. When it ended I didn't know what to do with myself.

The game got real meaning I was bound into a Stronghold of the mind. If you don't know what that is let me elaborate. A stronghold is a lie that Satan has established in our thinking that we count as truth. When we embrace those lies they affect our attitudes, emotions, and behavior. I believed this man was the one mainly because he looked and acted the part. And because he **told** me he was the one. Getting you to believe the lie by inserting a little bit of truth is the trick of the enemy. And, as I stated earlier, my nose was 'wide open'

You will have to break free physically. This means you must leave that man or thing alone. You will have to break free mentally. This means praying that God will bind that thing up to keep it away from you. And you will have to break free emotionally. Seek professional help, if need be. Find your happy place within you. *2nd Corinthians 10:3-5*

states, "For though we walk in the flesh, we do not war according to the flesh. For the weapons of our warfare are not carnal but mighty in God for pulling down strongholds, casting down arguments and every high thing that exalts itself against knowledge of God, bringing every thought into captivity to the obedience of Christ."

Sometimes we have been caught up in a generational curse that can get us bound up. We have be aware of that and cut that thing off at the root. Meaning that we are doing the same cycle momma, grandmomma, aunts and sisters may have dealt with regarding a man.

Chapter 6

You have to ask yourself, is it worth it? I became a broken woman. I didn't want a man to look, speak, or even breathe in my direction again. I must say, experience is a teacher, but do we learn the lesson? How many times will we need to repeat the lesson? Sometimes it takes us a couple of tries before we get it right, sisters. I know that from experience! We must be mindful at all times – especially if we have daughters. Let us have the wisdom and knowledge to educate our daughters and other women, whether young, middle-aged, or older. We must stick together as sisters in Christ!

This is not to say we are bashing men because we are speaking on this situation. In fact, this goes both ways – men and women need to know their worth. I don't mean being stuck up and hateful thinking that you are better than anybody else, displaying a hateful attitude. I simply mean that you should know your worth as a child of the King! Proverbs 4:23 "Above all else, guard your heart for everything you do flows from it."

Sisters you should make a checklist regarding your Boaz that you desire. Before you do that, make sure you know who and what a Boaz man is. You may need to read the book of Ruth. If you have not already read it, I suggest you do. It says quite a bit but I will only touch on it a little. Ruth 2:4-5 "Now behold, Boaz came from Bethlehem , and

said to the reapers, The Lord be with you! And they answered him, The Lord bless you! Then Boaz said to the servant who was in charge of the reapers , Whose young woman is this?" He saw the woman and was intrigued by who she was and how she carried herself. When you read the book of Ruth you will get the moral of the story of what type of man Boaz was and then you will understand.

Proverbs 18:22 states, "when a man findeth a wife he findeth a good thing and obtaineth favor with the Lord." Remember that it says when *HE* finds, not *she* finds. Matthew 19:5-6 "Therefore shall a man leave his father and mother and shall cleave unto his wife and they shall be one in flesh." Not two separate people doing what they want. "You do you and I'll do me," cannot happen if your marriage is of God. That's impossible because the two of you become one. There is no more individual – you are joined together.

The order should be God, Wife and Children! Also know and understand a real man doesn't *findeth* a "work-wife", side-chick, play-toy, bae or boo outside of his marriage! If you fall into one of those categories, Honey, you will be looking like boo boo the fool! What I mean by that is if he is already currently married he isn't the man for you. If he is already in a relationship or -ships, he cannot be your man. And let me say this... If he comes to you talking about the woman he is currently in a relationship with, KNOW that he will do the same to the next woman he encounters. That is usually a ploy to get with you because we women operate off our emotions. So sisters let that spirit of discernment and prayer kick in.

Chapter 7

We must always know who we are and whose we are! We must learn to love ourselves first! Have standards for a man that will pray for you, pray with you, build with, and grow with you. You don't have to settle for a meager male figure. If you have to supply everything from the roof, car and all the bills think about it... Sure, things happen and you might have to carry him for a minute depending on the situation. If you have to keep carrying him and being the provider for a male that is supposed to be a man, yet he isn't attempting to stand on his own two feet you need to drop that zero and wait on that hero!

So let me elaborate on what you have asked God for, You might have asked for a man with a six-figure salary, with his own business, house, and car. And that is great! Sometimes God might have a different plan for you. That is where you seek the Lord regarding that man. He might come along and not have any, or only some, of those things you asked for. That might be acceptable only if God says so because you two are too build all of the rest of that together. The key is God! Not your thoughts, but God's answer.

It might sound like I'm contradicting myself from the earlier statement that a King will have it all together when he comes to you. But, I'm really not. Quite often it isn't the material means, but the God in

him, the heart, the drive, the goals and the mindset of that man that proves he is the Boaz sent for you. If you are sick or hurt you shouldn't have to worry about eating. Your bills should be considered and gas should be in your car. He will make sure you have everything you need even if it takes away from his needs. That is a true man!

You shouldn't have to ask and definitely not beg. A real man will have the automatic response in his mind and heart to know he must take care of you if you are truly the woman he loves. I want to share another testimony with you. I met a man – or so I thought. He actually turned out just to be a male figure who had it all the money, his own house, and cars. He deceived me by telling me 'oh I'm tired of all of these women playing games, and I'm looking for that Godly woman who loves God and wants to get married ,and I fell for it so we got engaged and at first everything was fine but as we got closer to the wedding date he started acting crazy and then all of a sudden out of the blue he became verbally abusive and manipulating and said I don't want to get married I'd rather be by myself so I learned that he was a broken man who basically made me pay for what other women had done to him. I can share these life lessons now because I have grown and healed from them. I said that to say sometimes meeting a man with "everything" can be a bad situation as well.

My Sisters, do not let your loneliness lower your standards, ever! God wants you to have the best man, the God ordained man, He sent for you. That way He will be well pleased because we are His children. Believe God for everything! He wants us to have new life with all of the joy, love and understanding we can stand! If you walk with Him, He will walk with you. Psalm 37:4 "Delight yourself also in the Lord , and

He shall give you the desires of your heart." If it is in His will, you will have what you have prayed for. It took me a minute to understand and realize some of the things that I wanted were not of God and I'm grateful He corrected me. Always allow Him to be your teacher, correction and protection is a must with God.

Chapter 8

In Matthew 18:20 the word states "where there are two or more touching and agreeing in His name there He will be in the midst also." If you can't touch and agree on anything God is not in the midst! He does not dwell in mess. 1st Corinthians 14:33 His word states "God is not the author of confusion." Don't get it confused because every day may not be a good day. That is a normal life but your relationship with anyone should not be a life of misery and hell! We are not perfect. Only Jesus Christ is perfect. But that doesn't mean you have to constantly deal with negativity, abuse, and drama. That is living in bondage and God doesn't want that for you. Pray for the spirit of discernment ladies. That is very important! Trust me that it is the best thing to do if you are unsure in that relationship. If there is any inkling of doubt you may already have an answer. Proverbs 3:5-6 "Trust in the Lord with all thine heart, And lean not on your own understanding, In all your ways acknowledge Him, And He shall direct your path."

This is very dear, so I want to make this very clear to you. **PLEASE** never, *ever*, think less of yourself in any way! Do not think that you must accept mental, physical, verbal, or emotional abuse just to say you have a man in your life! That is not the definition of a real man! That is a male figure who is struggling with his own demons and identity. You're just getting caught up in the crossfire.

I have heard people say 'oh he was upset,' or 'I made him mad,' or 'he will never do it again...' Stop fooling yourself!

IF HE HIT YOU ONCE HE WILL HIT YOU AGAIN!!!

IF HE HIT YOU ONCE HE WILL HIT YOU AGAIN!!!

IF HE HIT YOU ONCE HE WILL HIT YOU AGAIN!!!

That is not a man! That is a little boy who is weak and a coward. That is a very weak sad person. Most physical abusers more than likely have seen it or endured themselves. He may even think it "makes him a man" because he can control you. God did not make you a punching bag! If he thinks that is okay to hit you, that little fella is fighting some demons! Here comes the verbal abuse if he calls you every curse word and not your government name. When he talks to you like a dog or gives you no respect in front of anybody or behind closed doors. Next up is your emotional abuse constantly telling you that you are fat, ugly, and/or lazy. Or trying to dictate your appearance, or saying you can't do anything right, or he doesn't have time for you, or disrespects you in front of other people... When he won't listen and/or compromise. Beware of all of those negative spirits we have to realize we can take on other people spirits by being around them as well as laying with them. That is real trust and believe! This is not acceptable in any form or on any level. That male has no clue of what love is. I remember a quote saying, 'I'd rather have a lonely spot next to me than a bad spirit.' You have to remember you are a Jewel.

The man should love you as Christ loved the church Ephesians 5:25 states, "Husbands love your wives even as Christ also loved the church,

and gave himself for it." We must also learn that we can't stay with men or choose a man because we feel sorry for him. I honestly feel you shouldn't stay because you have children together. Now, don't quote me as saying 'get a divorce' or 'leave him.' I'm just letting you know the consequences that come with that. Trust me, I have seen it first hand in my family. So I say all of that to say that you are not just scarring yourself but your children, as well. Keeping them in bondage in that toxic environment and in an unstable home is causing psychological trauma to all of you. You may convince yourself to stay in a toxic dead end relationship saying 'I just can't leave he needs me.' Believe me that isn't a relationship – that is a hardship that will eventually turn into a dictatorship from him.

Be careful! Use that spirit of discernment. The devil is very crafty. He knows us as well as God does. He knows what we like and will use that to try and tempt us. 1st Corinthians 10:13 "No temptation has overtaken you except such as is common to man; but God is faithful, who will not allow you to be tempted beyond what you are able, but with the temptation will also make the way of escape, that you will be able to bear it."

Chapter 9

Your mate should be your confidant, provider, protector and only lover. You should cherish, support and encourage one another. What I mean by that if he is sent by God you will know. You won't have to worry or wonder about him nor the relationship. You two stay in the will of God. Your relationship will flourish. You two should be able to talk about every and anything. You should agree to disagree, remembering that in anything communication is the key. Never let the sun go down without you resolving any conflicts and forgiving each other for any disagreements that you may have had earlier that day. Ephesians 4:26 states "Be ye angry and sin not: the sun go down upon your wrath."

You two should be so in tuned with each other that you feel each other when you aren't around one another. You can sense each other's emotions whether happy or sad. Be sure to have a man that is proud to have you and will do whatever it takes Godly too keep you. He will never risk losing the Queen God has blessed him with and vice versa. You two should have each others back in so many ways. You should want an "if you got it, he got it & if he got it, you got it" type of relationship! Never what's mine is mine and what's yours is yours. It doesn't work that way. Hence, it is why you become one once you are married. If a man does not see you as wife material he shouldn't see you

at all – point-blank-period! If he only sees you as someone to lay down with or use for his benefit in any type of way, that's a no-go. Know your worth!

As a side note for us women. Remember you have to carry yourself as a wife in order to be considered wife material. I have found that some of us get into relationships and stay in unhealthy relationships, or just situation-ships, because we don't want to be alone or just grow old alone. Some are looking for that father figure because your father wasn't in your life. Honestly, some of us didn't or don't know any better. I shall explain more about these issues in the next chapter, but the devil is a liar! That isn't God's plan for us. Proverbs 2:6 "For the Lord gives wisdom from His mouth and come knowledge and understanding."

The key to this book is to know your worth! Never settle for second best! Always pray for and desire the best of everything! If you don't that is where you fall short and wind up in the toxic, dead end, habitual and miserable relationships. A man is to honor you and vice versa. Be mindful of people making withdrawals in your life and never depositing anything good! That is out of balance and causes you to feel weary, used, tired, and taken for granted. These feelings can lead to a negative spirit, bitterness, vulnerabilities, and depressions. These are just a few things that can form from being used and hurt. No we may not be able to catch everything that isn't right but we definitely can be watchful and learn to seek God, which is your guide.

Chapter 10

My sister's prayer is really, really important. I cannot express that enough. You need to have a prayer partner on the same level or higher level to pray with you and for you. Make no mistake, you do have to be careful who you ask to pray for you. I found it is essential to your peace and health. Colossians 4:2-4 "Continue in prayer, and watch in the same with thanksgiving; With praying also for us, that God would open to us a door of utterance, to speak the mystery of Christ, for which I am also in bonds: That I may make it manifest, as I ought to speak." In a relationship you will have to walk by faith in some situations that may arise and are not in your control. Hebrews 11:1 "Now faith is the substance of things to hope for, the evidence of things not seen." Remember this as well with situations Philippians 4:6 "Be anxious for nothing, but in everything by prayer and supplication with thanksgiving let your request be known to God." With that being said, be mindful also of the things for which you are praying. Let not it be in vain or a repetitious prayer of something that will not honor God and give Him glory.

In a relationship it's best to always keep your business between three people – you, your mate and God. If you don't have God in it at all times there can be a crack in your foundation which will cause your house to crumble. In a relationship you must have honesty and loyalty

with much understanding. Nothing is ever one sided. If so, it is not of God and not for you.

Communication is the major key to developing a healthy relationship. let's elaborate on how that communication should work. Often in a situation one of the people involved may not be able to talk through the problem at that moment. This is understandable. But you cannot just walk away without saying 'can we talk about it later' or that 'I cannot speak on it at this time.' That is the proper and grown thing to do because nobody is a mind reader and assuming is never good! You have to learn each other and communicate on a daily basis to know each others likes and dislikes. Discuss your hopes and dreams with one another. Feed off of each other to grow and help one another succeed in life because life changes daily. Proverbs 27:17 states "Iron sharpens Iron."

Because one person will not communicate with the other things can go unsaid, time is wasted, and feelings are hurt. Life is entirely too short for child's play. If you are with someone say what you mean and mean what you say. But always be kind and understanding and remember everything isn't a joke to the other person. You have to have compassion and a listening ear to understand. If your mate can't give you that he isn't the man for you. He has some growing up to do.

Lets discuss trust. If you have no trust you have nothing! Believe me if you have the spirit of discernment you will know when a trust issues arises in the relationship. **ALWAYS** be truthful in everything, even if it will hurt the other person. It is best and respectful to tell the truth in the beginning than for them to find out later. So in all things get an understanding.

If you ask your mate something and they come out of the mouth with this statement "that's on a need to know basis..." you need to exit that so-called relationship! They are trying to hide something and that is their way of letting you know. They are also telling you that that will not change, and I say that because of experience. I was dating someone and that is what he told me when I asked a question about something that didn't quite seem right because of trust issues arising in our relationship. That stemmed from him always hollering privacy and getting up going outside to talk on certain calls. As I stated earlier that can happen. He was cheating and thought he was a ladies man. Let me elaborate on the word cheating. If you are sneaking to call, text, and/or spend time with someone else other than your mate and it's not your family or business partner (and I don't mean funny business, either), whether it is sexual or not, that is defined as cheating. Because if there isn't anything wrong going on you wouldn't have to sneak. You would be able to have that conversation in front of your mate. You wouldn't be hiding anything! So ladies don't accept that. If you ask something and he says 'it's a need to know basis,' you need to exit relationship because he is playing games. Let him play by himself! When you learn how much you are worth you will not settle for less! You will not just give your heart or your body to anybody.

I also want to share this with you. Yes, men and women can have friends of the opposite gender, but it should stay on a 'friend level.' No disrespect of any kind should be entertained. This can include text messages back and forth regarding sex, or him constantly coming and/ or going spend time with that person which is not their mate. It also includes calling and talking about how they miss them and asking if they are married yet or still single and ready to mingle. Now that can take

place because one grown person should have no absolute control over the action of another. But if your man does not correct the female that is a level of disrespect on both sides from him and her.

Also beware of these type of spirits such as the liar, lazy, sneaky, and cheating spirits. My Sisters, there are some good men out there. Just remember to be careful pray and ask God for that keen spirit of discernment and a sign. Please take heed – we need to love ourselves first! I cannot express that enough because I had to learn that the hard way. Sometimes we think we do love ourselves only to find out that we do not. We need to be watchful that if he isn't willing to go the extra mile for you then he isn't the one for you and vice versa in that situation.

Chapter 11

You may say what makes her think she has the answers to everything?!? Well, she doesn't. But she can share her story with you so that you will understand why she wrote this book. I hope it will help someone else who has been through, or is going through what I have endured in my life. Sometimes we are ashamed of our lessons learned. I don't call them mistakes; I call it a lesson. People come in our lives for a season, a reason, and a purpose. In times you need to know which is which and move on, never to do it again. Experience is *always* a teacher. We might be afraid of what others may think or say and sometimes we just don't know how to get out of the situation. But I'm here to share with you that God will bring you out! But you must want to be delivered from that situation. Only you know how much you can and want to deal with. Trust me if it is going back and forth, it's not of God. Remember He is not the author of confusion. Hebrews 12:2 "Looking unto Jesus the author and finisher of our faith; who for the joy that was set before him endured the cross, despising the shame , and set down at the right hand of the throne of God."

Okay ladies let me share some more of my story with you. Some may be able to relate and some may not but here we go. I will touch on some of the subjects from previous chapters. This is about that lonely spirit. I didn't want to be alone because I had abandonment issues from my childhood. My mother passed away when I was ten years old and

my father wasn't there in the first 15 years of my life so I felt all alone. I didn't feel loved and cared for as a child and I am emotionally scarred from somethings that happened in my life. I was looking for love in all of the wrong places. I became a mother at Eighteen years of age with a daughter not realizing I could pass that generational curse on to her. I got married six months after having my daughter to a man who was like a father to me – not a husband. First lesson learned because it was a very toxic and volatile marriage that ended quickly. Then two years later I had another baby. They were my world, not realizing I was still a baby myself while trying to take care of my own babies. In my mind I was no longer alone.

So it was me and my children against the world! I was going to church but still wasn't fully understanding God nor my worth so I entered into another relationship that was off and on for seven years. It got more toxic all the time. I was sacrificing more and more of me. I fell out of the will of God, not understanding that the man is to be the head of the house and to cover me. Sometimes I was having to be the head of the house and he was okay with that.

So, when that ended I begin to pray and ask God to show me a better way in life for me and my children. I was seeking to be in the will of God when I started going to church again. There is where I met and married my second husband.

Let me put this out there – I wasn't looking for a man because ladies we are not to go looking. Remember what the word of God says 'he that *findeth* a wife,' not *we go looking* for a husband. Let me say this, though, we need to know how to be a good God fearing and praying wife *BEFORE* you are found. I don't mean performing wifely duties to

the boyfriend! That is why your title is *girlfriend* not **wife** unless he puts a ring on it with a vow to God and you.

I learned that you need to be friends first but sometimes you will know he is the one that God has for you if you are in a relationship in tune with God the Father. I have heard people say 'well I have to try it before I buy it!' Nope, wrong answer! If it is in God's will for you it is already yours and compatible in all forms – so no need for a test drive!

Needless to say my second marriage ended we stopped communicating. As I said earlier in the book, if one little crack in the foundation is not addressed and fixed immediately, the whole house will crumble. As the years have gone by and I have grown I realized he wasn't sent by God. We were actually not in tune and on the same page. We actually put ourselves together so again communication is very important.

You also have to have a healthy balance in your relationship when you both work. There is a need to schedule things such as a date night at least once a week, and/or a quick getaway tripped planned once a month to stay connected at all times. The essence of balance is very much needed. As I stated earlier it is a commitment of two joined together as one. You are to share each other's dreams, talk daily about everything, and express your feelings and learn one another. But sisters the most important and main ingredient is allowing God to be the head of both of you.

And don't give up at the first sign of trouble! It easy seek help if **both** of you need and want to and try to work it out. But it does take the two of you to work through something. It cannot be done by one alone. If

it was ordained by God, He will fix it. Mark 10:9 "Therefore what God has joined together let no man separate." A strong prayer life is truly needed in any relationship but definitely in a marriage. That is a vow you take before God, each other and others.

Chapter 12

The divorce rate rises because we don't really take marriage seriously. Some people just want to say they are married or they just want the 45 minutes of the dresses, tuxedos and attention. But its work! Its not just 50/50, it's a 110/110 at all times! It takes God and the two of you that made that vow to make it work, but it will only work if it is in God's will. Again, not our will, but His will! I say this ladies know your situation and your worth because my issues caused me grief and pain. I became a broken woman all over again until God spoke to me and told me that He needed me to be alone to heal from my past and learn who I am and Whose child I am. Believe me it isn't easy, but if you don't heal and let go of that past it will follow you into every relationship that you try to have. It is an enduring process. It takes longer to heal the heart than to give the heart sometimes. I won't lie to you, for me it was a struggle. I've spent days crying, angry, confused, and wanting to give up – asking 'why me? What did I do wrong???' But then I started seeking God and started praying and I kept praying and trusting God through it all.

So I began to pray and commune with God on a daily basis. Realizing my worth and the Joy of the Lord was my strength brought me through. Psalm 17:8 "Keep me as the apple of Your eye ; hide me under

the shadow of your wings," meaning God protects us. He guards us, and once you learn that the other will come but you must be patient.

Let's talk about being yoked. There are two ways of being yoked together. Either you are evenly yoked or you are not. 2nd Corinthians 6:14 states, "Do not be unequally yoked together with unbelievers. For what fellowship has righteousness with lawlessness. And what communion has light with darkness?" Let me break that down for you. If the two of you cannot and will not be walking together in agreement, the weak one may be overtaken. For example, you go to church and he doesn't. If you are going to church and getting the word but not applying it to your life you are still weak and not progressing. You two are not on the same accord. Philippians 2:2 "Fulfill my joy by being like minded, having the same love, being of one accord, of one mind."

Scenario number two. You meet a man and he tells you he loves God and takes you to church and then you two start dating. Once he has you he stops serving God. You were never evenly yoked. It was just a ploy to get you into what will be a dysfunctional relationship. I'm speaking out of experience again. You need that spirit of discernment. God calls those type of people impostors – wolves in sheep's clothing seeking you out. So if you know that while dating them, you definitely don't want to marry them.

Now there have been some cases where one person was not saved and the other was and they got into a relationship and the other became saved. It can happen! Just be mindful to try the spirit by the spirit. 1John 4:1, "Dear friends, do not believe every spirit, but test the spirits to see whether they are from God, because many false prophets have

gone out into the world. 2 This is how you can recognize the Spirit of God: Every spirit that acknowledges that Jesus Christ has come in the flesh is from God, 3 but every spirit that does not acknowledge Jesus is not from God. This is the spirit of the Antichrist, which you have heard is coming and even now is already in the world."

Chapter 13

There are so many things to take into consideration here, so please read this very carefully.

Love has to be natural and unbiased. Either a person will show you and tell you, or they will leave you with assumptions to wonder. Don't change who you are and try to find someone to love you. If they love you then they would never want to see you go.

Love yourself first! Sometimes that can seem hard and lonely but it is much needed. If you don't love yourself how can you love someone else? Truly take the time and treat yourself properly that way you will definitely know if you are being treated correctly by someone else. If someone wants to show you they love you then allow them to do so. Don't make them feel that loving you is wrong.

You need to know that because a male wants to lay with you and talk about sex constantly, that isn't love. A person who loves you breaks down their own walls with no intention to rebuild the walls that fell. A person that truly wants to change and truly wants you will show you just as much as you show them. I have also experienced some people who want to try to love others but don't properly know how. If they really don't know how they may not truly understand love. They may hear it and see it from other people and may have even been taught

somethings, but not enough. They may not have been taught how to be a man who fully grasps the concept of how to show love properly.

These words reminded me of the time I asked God to change my heart because I was so tired of being hurt by others. I asked God to take away my loving, giving heart. The Holy Spirit convicted me so quick I had to do a self-check-up and go back and apologize to God for that stupid foolish request! God made me! I should not ever want to change because others have issues within themselves. Not for anyone, but especially if it is in regards to a man. 1st Timothy 4:4, states "For every creature of God is good, and nothing is to be refused if it is received with Thanksgiving." So I had to realize I was made that way by God for a reason.

Now it doesn't mean that I should allow people to hurt me or treat me any kind of way because of their shortcomings. I had to learn to be thankful for my loving, kind heart and to continue to be the loving person God made. I had to learn to watch as well as pray for myself to have the spirit of discernment. I learned how not to get caught up with people who wouldn't be good for me. Sometimes you don't know people until you have been around them. Always be mindful of what to look for while in their company,

Chapter 14

Let's discuss being spiritually bound together. We'll look at a wonderful example of the way a Queen should be treated. My Grandparents met when they were very young. They were married for over fifty years, until 'death did them part.' They met, fell in love, married and had children through out those fifty-plus years. Everyday wasn't always peaches and cream, but the love was always obviously present.

I had the opportunity and pleasure at a very young age to see a Queen in her element. I didn't realize how much of a blessing that was until later in my life. I was able to see this beautiful display of love from them until their dying end. My grandfather treated my grandmother like the (not 'a', but 'THE') Queen. I never heard him utter a hateful word towards her. I never saw any type of violence toward her.

He wasn't a highly-educated man and back in those days a higher level education wasn't required to earn a decent living. Everyday he got up and went to work to provide for his family. He worked hard for the Love of his life. He was the provider and protector in all ways. She didn't have to worry about bills transportation, food, or clothing – it was always provided for her. She really didn't have to work at all if she didn't want to. This is not to focus only on the finances, though. It was simply the consideration that they showed each other.

His desire was to always please her! Whether it was candy, cards, and/or gifts, it was always the biggest and the best for his Queen! He spoiled her. It was always about her. She never wanted for anything. Nothing stopped him when it came to maintaining her happiness. Now he didn't cook or clean, but she never stressed over anything. I never saw him show any level of disrespect to her. And if you had an issue with his Queen, "you better had come correct!"

They went to church together! Let me say that again because its the basis, foundation, and strength of their lasting marriage. They went to church **TOGETHER!** They served the Lord **TOGETHER!** They worshiped **TOGETHER!** They prayed for each other and their children and grandchildren **TOGETHER!** They did just about everything together. They believed that God had put them together for life.

They raised their children and lived life to the fullest! They showed me that "old-school, down-home" kind of love; the kind that isn't just for show. They showed me the real "I'm with you & I'm with you" kind of love! They were the true epitome of their vows 'through sickness & health, whether richer or poorer, until death do you part.'

What a terrific example my Grandparents are for modern-day marriages. Because of their godliness and earnest commitment to God and to each other, their love was amplified. Men and women around them couldn't help but notice, and their relationship stood the test of time.

A holy couple, joined in marriage, studying God's Word together, can slowly become a spiritual force in a world that desperately needs spiritually strong people. Can you imagine this kind of spiritual connection in your own marriage? Bible reading is one of the best ways to head in that direction and praying together daily you should be able to

know when something is wrong or out of sorts with the other because you have become spiritually connected. You are to pray for your mate daily. You should be their peace. Whatever storms arise you two should fight that battle together. But don't leave God out! He must always be a part that will ensure the connection. Nothing will bring two hearts together, than two hearts that are after God's heart.

What does it mean to cherish your spouse?

God created everyone different – this includes you and your spouse. He created each of us to have unique characteristics as part of his design plan. When we cherish our spouse, we appreciate and treasure those unique characteristics and can love them and our Creator in a more meaningful way. What is important to one may not seem to be import-ant to the other but that isn't the way you should treat each other. We were made differently – emotionally, physically, and mentally, but the love, desire, attention and caring should be equally for your spouse. It is true that whoever lives in love lives in God and God lives in them. The love that you two have should be so strong that years from now you will still be in love and not just love one another.

There is a difference between being in love and just loving one an-other. Loving someone is about how they make you feel. Being in love is about how you make them feel. Loving someone means you are only concerned with how he makes you feel loved, special, or appreciated. Being in love means you are more concerned about how ensuring that they feel loved and cherished. Being in love is like a breath of fresh air each and everyday you are with them and wanting the absolute best of everything for them. If you can say well I fell out of love then that probably means you were never really in love in the first place. Love is a

constant connection and must for the two people who have intertwined their two souls together in love.

This book is to help women of all ages, color and religious background to understand and know your worth regarding not just a man, but also life. We get so caught up in what others have and say. But you have to be careful. Because we are on the outside looking in we don't know that everything doesn't always seem to be what it looks like in every relationship. And then we don't really understand what we need, desire and and require for ourselves because we are too busy trying to live like someone else.

Chapter 15

I'm wrapping this book up ladies. I have shared some of my life experiences and some wisdom and knowledge lessons that I have learned. Some of these lessons I had to learn over and over (and over) again, so we will do a small recap of why this book was written. Prayerfully it will help my sisters along the way if you should run into any of the males that I have written about. I pray that it will help you recognize the man God has for you.

Let us beware and stay away from those foul spirits. Such as the male that needs a place to rest his head, or needs a car to drive that he doesn't pay the note on while he's "looking for a job." Or such as the ultimate ladies man trying to be a man but is really a boy. Be wise of his words. Don't get all silly and giggly because he says something nice to you, like 'baby you sure can cook and I'm so proud of you!' If you know who you are and Whose you are, you already know what you can do. Remember you were validated by the main man – God himself!

Well you need to look at him and see if there is anything you can be proud of in him. But this is a two way street. We may have brought with us the spirits of loneliness, or of over-mothering to the point of smothering. Or possibly a spirit of needing to be wanted because we lacked that father figure in our lives as a little girl.

Or we may have a lustful spirit that stems from low self esteem. It may sound like an old wives tale, but this it is true; what we allow is what we get. Some of us have lustful spirits! We must be mindful that while we are entertaining that clown at the circus we missed our King! The same king that was created and put on this earth just for you! The one that will treat you as the Queen you were born to be!

Let me say this disclaimer; this is not a book to bash the male figure! This is a book to help prevent or help rescue women out of a situation that you may not realize that you are in or know how to get out of. Because at one point that was me and I did not find a book like this to help me find myself in God and God in me.

My Sisters, watch as well as pray about the dude that jumps in your inbox on social media, that you ran into at the gym, or the grocery store, or (sad to say) at the church house. Sit back and observe. Talk to God! Start praying about that male and ask the holy spirit to reveal to you if this man is a King or a clown. Trust me, I have learned that if you are sincere in your prayer, God will reveal it and you will be amazed!

OH, I almost forgot this tidbit... I meant to say it earlier on in the book, but no, maybe this is the right place. This way it will be the last thing you read, but the first thing that you think about when you meet that male. If he cannot or will not look you in the eye when you communicate, he is **NOT** a true man! I'm sure you have heard the eyes are the window to the soul? But I have found some can be and still are not

good for you. With the spirit of disce [...] [...]y[...] you will be able to tell when the eyes have it.

I pray that God blesses all of my beautiful Sisters reading this! My Sisters prepare to meet the love of your life!